FRANCESCO GIOIA

^{The}Apostle Paul

The Testimony of Joy amidst Suffering

Libreria Editrice Vaticana

Translation from the Italian:
John A. Abruzzese.

*Libreria Editrice Vaticana:
www.libreriaeditricevaticana.com

ISBN 88-209-4576-2

Cover:
Fresco of St. Paul, Antoniazzo Romano,
Patriarchal Basilica of St. Paul - Rome.

Back Cover:
Arms of St. Paul, Cloister of the Patriarchal
Basilica of St. Paul - Rome.

* The illustrations are from the series of 36 frescoes (1857-1860),
narrating the life of the Apostle Paul, in the Patriarchal Basilica
of St. Paul (Rome).

GAGLIARDI PIETRO (1809-1890)

Conversion of Saul (Acts 9: 1-9)

Introduction

The indisputable search for joy is verified in every thought and action in a person's life. Simply stated, it can be said to be the purpose of human existence. St. Augustine insists that "the spirit is nourished by what gives it joy"[1] and "it is impossible to find a single person who does not desire happiness."[2]

Pascal comments on the subject: "Without exception, each person seeks to be happy. Whatever means is employed, all tend to this end. The cause which makes some want to go to war, and others to avoid it, is the same desire in both, but with varying vantage points. The will never makes the slightest move without this goal in mind. This is the basis of each person's every action, even those who take their own life."[3] It can be concluded, then, that, notwithstanding all the miseries of human life, "a person wishes to be happy and cannot wish not to be so."[4]

Having been born for joy, each person has only one task: to be happy. Not to be happy is the ultimate betrayal.

---

[1] SAINT AUGUSTINE, *Confessions*, XIII, 27 ("*Inde quippe animus pascitur, unde laetatur*").

[2] SAINT AUGUSTINE, *Sermons*, LIII.

[3] PASCAL, *Pensées*, 425.

[4] PASCAL, *ivi*, 169. Alphonse Goettmann states that "joy makes the individual in the same manner as a stream arises from its source. Where the distant meanderings of a stream might lead to obscuring any idea of the source, the person, in his wanderings, can also forget the Essential (...). A person cannot live, however, without joy; life can only triumph where joy is present." (*La gioia, volto di Dio nell'uomo* ["Joy, the Face of God in Man"], San Paolo, Cinisello Balsamo, 2003, pp. 17-18).

By its very nature, joy is an essential part of the biblical message. The same is true of the Apostle Paul, who, if not "the second founder of Christianity"[5] as Wilhelm Wrede (1859-1906) maintains, certainly stands out as a man of great importance.

Paul uses the words "grace and peace" as a greeting to his hearers at the beginning and end of all his letters,[6] thereby setting a joyous tone.

Paul always approaches the subject of joy by way of exhortation. His constant appeal to his hearers is: "Be happy" (cháirete).[7] It is an imperative in the present tense, which means that Christian joy is a continuous condition in life and not limited to a fleeting moment.

It has been observed that Paul's letters "do not contain a theological treatise on joy like that on faith, hope and charity. Christian joy permeates all of Paul's theology."[8]

Paul links the subject of joy to salvation. His reason rests in the fact that human beings are constitutionally unhappy. God, however, in his goodness and almighty power, takes humanity out of this state of unhappiness, that is, he saves humankind. Consequently, "salvation and happiness seem to coincide conceptually. Even if it be in an indirect way, the biblical doctrine of salvation is for Israel the only authentic response to the age-old problem of human happiness."[9]

Drawing upon our previous work, Nati per la gioia *("Born for Joy") (Ancora, Milano 2004), we*

---

[5] W., WREDE, *Paulus* (Paul), Tübingen 1904, p. 104.

[6] Only the Letter to the Hebrews does not open with this greeting; it does appear however in its closing.

[7] Cf. I Thess. 5:16; 2 Cor 13:11; Phil 3: 1; 4:4.

[8] N. BEAUPÈRE, *San Paolo e la gioia. Il messaggio di speranza* ("St. Paul and Joy: the Message of Hope"), Città Nuova, Roma 1975, p. 30.

[9] A. MATTIOLI, *Beatitudini e felicità nella Bibbia d'Israele* ("Blessedness and Happiness in the Bible of Israel"), Città Nuova, Firenze 1992, p. 9.

gather in the work which follows various stones in the mosaic of joy found in the letters of St. Paul,[10] with the intention of making the "Apostle to the Gentiles" better known, even among unbelievers, as he states himself;[11] and to be with him "coworkers of joy"[12] in the lives of others, particularly those who often find themselves in hopeless situations and those who are given to sadness, depression and pessimism.

+ Francesco Gioia, *Archbishop*
Pontifical Administrator of
the Patriarchal Basilica of St. Paul

Rome, 29 June 2004 , *The Solemnity of Saints Peter and Paul*

---

[10] Tradition has attributed 14 letters to St. Paul. Recent scholarship, however, points to the fact that the Letter to the Hebrews is not from Paul's hand. Among the remaining 13 letters, the "7 great letters" (1 Thessalonians, 1-2 Corinthians, Galatians, Romans, Philippians, Philemon) have never been placed in doubt. 2 Thessalonians can also be placed with these, even if many consider it a "pseudo-work," a common occurrence in classical literature where public opinion attributes a text to a given author. The Letter to the Philippians and that to Philemon are also called "letters from prison," because tradition holds that they were written during Paul's imprisonment in Rome at the beginning of 60 A.D.. 1-2 Timothy and the Letter to Titus, called the "pastoral epistles," namely written to pastors, are considered "post-Pauline," that is, "pseudo-works." Some raise doubts concerning Paul's authorship of Colossians and Ephesians. Paul wrote the First Letter to the Thessalonians from Corinth in 50 A.D. or 51 A.D. at the latest. A few months later he wrote the Second Letter. From a chronological perspective, these two letters are the first writings of the New Testament.

[11] Rm 11:13; cf. 15, 16, 18; Acts 18:6; 22:21; 26:20; Gal 1: 16; 2:2, 8-9; Col 1:27; 1Thess 2:16; 1 Tim 2:7; 3:16.

[12] 2 Cor 1:24.

DE SANCTIS GUGLIELMO (1829-1911)

Saul flees from Damascus (Acts 9: 22-25)

1. "You are our glory and joy" [13]

The Letters to the Thessalonians present a community which has scarcely accepted the new faith, where the newcomers still manifest an enthusiasm typical of converts. Referring to those days, the Apostle states: "You became imitators of us and of the Lord, for you received the word in much affliction, with joy inspired by the Holy Spirit; so that you became an example to all the believers in Marcedonia and in Achaia." [14]

In this passage, Paul reveals three elements related to Christian joy: joy results from accepting the Word; joy is present in suffering; and joy is a gift of the Holy Spirit.

Because Paul was forced to flee Thessalonica, [15] he was unable to follow first-hand the development of the new community. However, his spirit is overflowing with serenity and peace, when he comes to know that "not only has the word of the Lord sounded forth from you in Macedonia and Achaia, but your faith in God has gone forth everywhere. [16]

The suffering and distance caused by forced separation does not overshadow the happiness which the Apostle experiences in seeing the Thessalonians persevere in the faith. He is happy not for the success of his apostolic activity, but for the seriousness with which these people have welcomed and lived

---

[13]   1 Thess 2:20.
[14]   1 Thess 1:6-7.
[15]   Cf. Acts 17:10.
[16]   1 Thess 1:8.

the Gospel. It is for them that he rejoices: "For what is our hope or joy or crown of boasting before our Lord Jesus at his coming? Is it not you? For you are our glory and joy."[17]

To obtain information about the Thessalonians, Paul sent Timothy to strengthen them in the faith they received and to exhort them not to be moved by the afflictions they were enduring. The "good news" reported by Timothy once again fills his heart with joy. He then writes: "For what thanksgiving can we render to God for you, for all the joy which we feel for your sake before our God, praying earnestly night and day that we may see you face to face and supply what is lacking to your faith?"[18]

The joy of the Thessalonians is the joy typical of every believer. The joy of Paul is the joy of an Apostle and the joy of a mother and a father.[19] It is a joy which exults in the happiness of children who have been begotten in the faith of Christ.[20] Bidding his hearers farewell, Paul urges them to live in peace, harmony, charity and patience; but he also calls them to a Christian joy of which they have tasted the first fruits: "Rejoice always."[21] This is the command he leaves to the members of the young Church.

Saint Basil the Great, referring to St. Paul's exhortation, asks himself: "For what is virtuous, they say, about passing one's life in gladness of soul, in joy and good cheer night and day? And how is it possible to achieve this,

---

[17]   1 Thess 2:19-20.
[18]   1 Thess 3:9-10.
[19]   Cf. 1 Thess 2:6-8, 11.
[20]   Cf. 1 Cor 4:5; Gal 4:19; Philemon 10.
[21]   1 Thess 5:16.

when we are beset by countless unexpected evils, which create unavoidable dejection in the soul? In such a case, it is no more feasible for us to rejoice and be of good cheer than for one who is being roasted on a gridiron not to feel agony or for one who is being goaded not to suffer pain... How is it possible for me always to rejoice, one may ask, when I have no grounds for being joyous? For the factors that cause rejoicing are external and do not reside within us. ... How is it, therefore, that a commandment has been given to us that cannot be accomplished by our own choice, but depends on other antecedent factors?"

According to St. Basil, the response to this question is seen in the intention of the Apostle. He continues: "in attempting to elevate our souls from the earth to the heights and to transport ourselves to a heavenly way of life ... For his part, the Apostle summons not just anyone, but one who is as he was, to rejoice always, by no longer living in the flesh but having Christ living in him. Indeed, union with the highest good does not in any way take account of the demands of the flesh. ... a soul which has once and for all been held fast by the desire for its Creator and is accustomed to delighting in the beauties of the heavenly realm will not diminish its great joy and cheerfulness under the influence of carnal feelings, which are varying and unstable; but it will regard the things which distress other people as a means of increasing its own gladness. Such was the case in the Apostle's life; he took pleasure in infirmities, afflictions, persecutions and necessities, counting his needs as an occasion for glorying."[22]

---

[22] SAINT BASIL THE GREAT, *Homily on Thanksgiving*, 2.

The teaching on the *parousia*, that is, "the Lord's Second Coming," "troubled" the Thessalonians. To calm their concerns the Apostle offers a timely "clarification" and a heartfelt exhortation to perseverance.[23] In the end, he calls upon God to comfort all the members of the community: "May our Lord Jesus Christ himself, and God our Father, who loved us and gave us eternal comfort and good hope through grace, comfort your hearts and establish them in every good work and word."[24] Faith is not abstract talk but good works, which are the source of consolation and comfort for the believer.

If, in his first letter, Paul exhorts the brethren of Thessalonika to joy, in the second he pleas that "the Lord of peace" grant them this gift and the joy which is inseparable from it: "peace at all times and in all ways."[25]

---

[23] Cf. 2 Thess 2:1-15.
[24] 2 Thess 2:16-17.
[25] 2 Thess 3:16.

TOJETTI DOMENICO (1831-1901)

Paul in Corinth (*Acts* 18: 1-4)

2. "We work with you for your joy" [26]

The subject of joy is treated many times in the Letters to the Corinthians. Among the Christians of Corinth some are demanding, quarrelsome, restless and even permissive. Before exhorting them to rejoice, Paul calls them to right conduct, humility, harmony and a charity which never "rejoices" in wrong-doing. [27]

Afterwards, he responds directly to their questions and emphasizes the fleeting nature of human existence and the fragility of the satisfactions which it offers: "those who mourn" ought to live "as though they were not mourning and those who rejoice as though they were not rejoicing," because "the appointed time has grown very short and the form of this world is passing away." [28]

Ezechial, anticipating the fall of Jerusalem and Judea, said: "The time has come, the day draws near. Let not the buyer rejoice, nor the seller mourn, for wrath is upon all their multitude." [29] In this context, Paul's advice to a widow is that "it is better," namely, there is more joy (*makariotéra*), if she remains as she is. [30]

The Apostle does not deny the validity of earthly joy, but he encourages people to resist the temptation of considering it as an end in itself and not to forget its fleeting character which can change joy into sorrow. Indirectly, he asks people to seek the joy of God which is eternal.

---

[26] 2 Cor 1:24.
[27] 1 Cor 13:6.
[28] 1 Cor 7: 29-31.
[29] Ezechial 7:12.
[30] Cf. 1 Cor 7:40.

Evil plagues human existence but evil can be overcome in Christ: "But thanks be God, who give us the victory through our Lord Jesus Christ!"[31]

Paul, who was originally uplifted by the good news received from Thessalonika, is now saddened by what is told him about the behaviour of some Corinthians on various occasions.[32] Nevertheless, even here he finds a reason for joy in the visit of some of the faithful of that community: "I rejoice at the coming of Stephanus and Fortunatus and Achaicus, because they have made up for your absence; for they refreshed my spirit as well as yours. Give recognition to such men."[33]

Joy abounds in those who are in contact with joyous people: "if one member is honoured, all rejoice together."[34]

In his Second Letter to the Corinthians Paul states, with surprising incisiveness, that God bestows joy in a special way on those who suffer, a joy which by its nature must be shared with others: "Blessed be the God and Father of our Lord Jesus Christ, the Father of mercies and the God of all comfort, who comforts us in all our affliction, so that we may be able to comfort those who are in any affliction, with the comfort with which we ourselves are comforted by God. For as we share abundantly in Christ's sufferings. So through Christ we share abundantly in comfort too. If we are afflicted, it is for your comfort and salvation, and it we are comforted, it is for your comfort, which you experience when you patiently endure the same sufferings

---

[31] 1 Cor 15:57.
[32] Cf. 1 Cor 5:2; 6:5; 11:17.
[33] 1 Cor 16: 17-18.
[34] 1 Cor 12:26.

that we suffer. Our hope for you is unshaken; for we know that as you share in our sufferings, you will also share in our comfort."[35]

Helping the faithful be aware of this comforting reality is part of the Apostle's mission. In this regard, he recalls once again that the Corinthians are present in his heart "to die together and to live together."[36]

To have compassion for someone who is suffering is natural, but to be a coworker of joy for others requires a particular sensitivity and a precise commitment. The Second Vatican Council urged the disciples of Christ to make their own not only "the griefs and anxieties of the world", but also "its joys and hopes."[37] In the past, "ascetic teaching was centred exclusively on the sufferings of humanity. We were specialists in the art of compassion. Our spirituality was influenced by the irresistible appeal of the Cyrenian who bore the cross. But the masters of the interior life did not so much as give a thought to the idea that there might also be Cyrenians who bear joy."[38]

In taking account of his difficulties, Paul refers to the trials to which he and his pastoral activity were subjected;[39] nevertheless he says with a certain satisfaction: "We are sorrowful, but always rejoicing."[40] In this way, he displays

---

[35] 2 Cor 1:3-7.

[36] 2 Cor 7:3.

[37] SECOND VATICAN ECUMENICAL COUNCIL, The Pastoral Constitution on the Church in the Modern World *Gaudium et Spes*, 1.

[38] T. BELLO, *Cirenei della gioia* ("Cyrenians of Joy"), San Paolo, Cinisello Balsamo 1995, pp. 13-14; J. RATZINGER prefers to speak of *Servitore della vostra gioia* ("Servants of Our Joy"), Àncora, Milano 1989.

[39] Cf. 2 Cor 6:3-9; 11:22-33.

[40] 2 Cor 6:10.

a characteristic feature of the Christian life: to be in possession of a deep sense of joy, despite apparent sadness, a joy which can be noted on his face, in his voice and in his words.

To the members of the "Church of God which is at Corinth and all who are in the whole of Achaia" he writes: "For we do not want you to be ignorant, brethren, of the affliction we experienced in Asia; for we were so utterly, unbearably crushed that we despaired of life itself. Why, we felt that we had received the sentence of death." At the same time, he relates the lesson learned in suffering: "we have learned not to rely on ourselves but on God who raises the dead; he delivered us from so deadly a peril, and he will deliver us; on him we have set our hope that he will deliver us again."[41]

He accepts every trial for the love of Christ, "for Christ's sake," to use his own words: "We are fools for Christ's sake.... We hunger and thirst, we are ill-clad and buffeted and homeless, and we labour, working with our own hands. When reviled, we bless; when persecuted, we endure; when slandered, we try to conciliate; we have become, and are now, as the refuse of the world, the offscouring of all things."[42]

Paul resolves the present woes by looking to the future in store for the faithful: "We are afflicted in every way, but not crushed; perplexed, but not driven to despair; persecuted but not forsaken; struck down, but not destroyed; always carrying in the body the death of Jesus, so that the life of Jesus may also be manifested in our bodies."[43] "If we have died with him, we shall also live with him."[44]

---

[41] 2 Cor 1:1, 8-10; cf. Acts 19:23-41.
[42] 1 Cor 4:10-13.
[43] 2 Cor 4:8-10.
[44] 2 Tim 2:11.

This certainty comes from faith in God: "(we know) that he who raised the Lord Jesus will raise us also with Jesus and bring us with you into his presence.... So we do not lose heart. Though our outer nature is wasting away, our inner nature is being renewed every day. For this slight momentary affliction is preparing for us an eternal weight of glory beyond all comparison, because we look not to the things that are seen but to the things that are unseen; for the things that are seen are transient, but the things that are unseen are eternal."[45] In another place he states: "I consider that the sufferings of this present time are not worth comparing with the glory that is to be revealed to us."[46] Paul gives a testimony of joy amidst suffering.

The afflictions abounding in his life are borne for the same reason that Christ bore his sufferings: in defence of truth and justice. Consequently, they may weaken the body but not the spirit; they do not diminish his enthusiasm but, instead, bring him comfort and courage.[47] He expressly likens his life to that of Christ who suffered for others. In the same way Christ suffered for the happiness of his "children," Paul transmits to the Corinthians the entire Christian message without accommodating their "lofty" preconceptions[48] and without being intimidated by their expectations.

The difficulties arising from the superficial character of the Corinthians saddened Paul, but it did not distance him from them. He suffered; but his suffering served to make their faith stronger and to deepen his love for them. In this manner, it lead to mutual consolation.

---

[45] 2 Cor 4: 14, 16-17; cf. Rm 6:5.
[46] Rm 8:18; 1 Pt 5:10; cf. Wisdom 3:5.
[47] Cf. 2 Cor 4:7-18.
[48] Cf. 1 Cor 2:1-5.

Paul loved the Corinthians. If they had troubled him by their impertinence, he bore no resentment against anyone. If he did not return to Corinth, it was to "save" them from reproof, so as not to exacerbate their spirits: "For I made up my mind not to make you another painful visit. For if I cause you pain, who is there to make me glad but the one whom I have pained? And I wrote as I did, so that when I came I might not be pained by those who should have made me rejoice, for I felt sure of all of you, that my joy would be the joy of you all."[49]

On this subject Hans U. Von Balthasar observes: "This risk of reaping joy in sadness and the sowing of the seeds of joy in the process, is very much alien to Old Testament logic. It is however an accepted part of the logic of Christ and his Cross. Such an action is the reflection of the attitude of Christ who carries his followers with him to the cross and expects them to understand the 'teaching' ('I am the way') of joy which is motivated by the cross and focussed on the cross."[50]

Paul has a deep affection for the faithful of Corinth and they know it: "Not that we lord it over your faith; we work with you for your joy."[51] The Apostle has no intention of "condemning anyone" but only of dispelling their anxiety, thereby, making them happy. Again he bares his soul: "I do not say this to condemn you, for I said before that you are in our hearts, to die together and to live together. I have great confidence in you; I have great pride in you; I

---

[49] 2 Cor 2:1-3.
[50] HANS URS VON BALTHASAR, *Joy and the Cross, Concilium* 1968, 9, p. 45.
[51] 2 Cor 1:24.

am filled with comfort. With all our affliction, I am overjoyed."[52]

St. John Chrysostom comments in this matter: "Paul, showed his magnanimity by not only declaring *I am overjoyed*, but adding, *in all our affliction*. For the delight you gave me was so great that no affliction could diminish it. Indeed, my abounding joy made me forget the sorrows which weighed me down and kept me from remaining downcast."[53]

Paul draws comfort from the visit of Titus and the good news he bore about this community. In this regard, the Apostle expressly states: "God, who comforts the downcast, comforted us by the coming of Titus, and not only by his coming but also by the comfort with which he was comforted in you." To have known of the Corinthians' "affection" for him, their "longing" to see him again and their "mourning" for the wrongs against him is enough to make him say: "I rejoiced still more."[54]

The preceding letter, "written with many tears,"[55] had caused the Corinthians to see the error of their ways. As a result, Paul happily adds: "As it is, I rejoice, not because you were grieved, but because you were grieved into repenting; for you felt a godly grief, so that you suffered no loss through us. For godly grief produces a repentance that leads to salvation and brings no regret, but worldly grief produces death."[56]

The Apostle's behaviour was not aimed at compensating for the offense, nor punishing the

---

[52]   2 Cor 7:3-4.
[53]   SAINT JOHN CHRYSOSTOM, *Homily on the Second Letter to the Corinthians*, 14, 2.
[54]   2 Cor 7:6-7.
[55]   2 Cor 2:4.
[56]   2 Cor 7:9-10.

offender, but to reestablishing good relations with the community. And when he achieved his goal, he was happy. "Here is what comforts us," he clearly confesses. At the same time, he goes further: "And besides our own comfort we rejoiced still more at the joy of Titus, because his mind has been set at rest by you all."[57] Paul rejoices at the newfound trust among the faithful at Corinth, manifested in not only their welcoming Titus, but, above all, their following his recommendations. He begged them: "Open your hearts to us." And with the return of peace, their understanding and former affection created an atmosphere of serenity and joy. The Apostle therefore exclaims with a certain pride: "I rejoice, because I have perfect confidence in you."[58]

The Christian vocation is characterized by not only the cross but also joy. Each does not exclude the other; they are united. The Church of Macedonia, despite its numerous trials, abounded in "great joy"; its "extreme poverty" did not stand in the way of the faithful's generosity towards the brothers of Jerusalem.[59]

The community of Corinth will continue to be of concern to Paul, but it will no longer pose a problem for him. He is sure of his mission; his good example will bring them along. Though some, roused by those who call themselves "superlative apostles,"[60] might again offend him and, forgetting humility and repentance, grow self-important, the words exchanged do not alter the situation. Examining themselves before Christ and assessing the situation in the light of faith bring knowledge of who is right. What

---

[57]   2 Cor 7:13.
[58]   2 Cor 7:2,16.
[59]   Cf. 2 Cor 8:2.
[60]   Cf. 2 Cor 12:11.

is important is that they choose to do good. Winning or losing has little importance.[61]

In his own case, Paul also "rejoices" in his weakness, that is, in accepting failure, so that the Corinthians might be strong in truth and goodness.[62] Above all, inner peace, serenity and joy must prevail: "Brethren, be happy, hold to perfection, encourage one another, agree with one another, live in peace and the God of love and peace will be with you."[63]

Christian behaviour is distinguished by acting rightly, doing good, and serenely accepting whatever sacrifice is required, because "God loves a cheerful (*hilarón*) giver."[64]

St. John Chrysostom develops Paul's thought in the following manner: "Why are you saddened at doing works of mercy and thereby renounce the fruit of your good work? If you are sad, you are not merciful, but brash and insensitive. In such a saddened state, how can you cheer up a person who is experiencing sorrow? It is desirable that in giving your gift with joy, the receiver has no ill conception, since nothing so humiliates a person as to receive from others. If your unmeasured joy does not dispel such a thought and you seem to be looking to receive rather than give, you burden the one who receives your gift rather than raising his spirits. ... Thus, in giving just a little in joy, you can give much; however, giving much in sadness can make the "much" you give of little worth."[65]

Where the above considerations can be reasons for joy among Christ's followers, the

---

[61]   Cf. 2 Cor 13:5-7
[62]   Cf. 2 Cor 13:9.
[63]   2 Cor 13:11.
[64]   2 Cor 9:7.
[65]   SAINT JOHN CHRYSOSTOM, *Homily on the Letter to the Romans*, 22, 1-2.

supreme reason for Paul is the resurrection of Christ, the mystery which also gives Christian joy its novelty. "Easter is the source of Christian joy. For the first Christians and for Christians of all times, there is no joy except in the resurrection of Christ. Such a joy is fundamentally different from all other religious and profane expressions of joy."[66]

A spirit of expectation does not exclude true happiness, since hope is assured in Jesus Christ, the "first-born of many brothers,"[67] "the first-born from the dead."[68] In going before his disciples into the kingdom of the Father, he prepared a place for them.[69] There he waits to seat them at his table, the traditional symbol of happiness.[70] In this context, joy in this life is a prefiguration of the happiness to come.

St. Paul reminds the Corinthians that if the resurrection did not take place, believers would be the most unhappy people in the world.[71] Without it, human existence would end in bitterness and despair, because undoubtedly, even in the best of situations, "the days of a good life are counted."[72]

Each life inevitably has its share of solitude, fear, desolation, discouragement and misfortune. The difference for the Christian is a joyful hope for a better future. The Church was born on Calvary through the paschal mystery of Christ. Where Paul recalls for his hearers

---

[66] N. BEAUPÈRE, *San Paolo e la gioia, op. cit.* ("St. Paul and Joy"), p. 45.
[67] Rm 8:29.
[68] Col 1:18.
[69] John 14:3.
[70] Cf. Luke 22:18.
[71] Cf. 1 Cor 15:19.
[72] Sirach 41:13.

that he bears in his body the passion of Christ, always and everywhere,[73] he does not tire also to propose the message of the resurrection as a source of joy.[74] He therefore associates joy and hope, appealing to his hearers to "rejoice in hope."[75]

Life's many trials call for courage and strength. Hope alone can bring joy, because it serves to inspire a person to look to the future where the shadows will be dispersed by light. St. Basil the Great states: "Hope makes joy dwell in the soul of the virtuous man."[76]

Hope is not simply the soul's longing or a human ambition, but a divinely grounded conviction in the "God of hope," who fills the heart with "every joy and peace."[77] Paul gives Christian hope a firm basis: "Hope does not disappoint us, because God's love has been poured into our hearts through the Holy Spirit who has been given to us."[78]

To emphasize the bond between joy and hope, the *Pastor of Hermes* uses an eloquent metaphor. He tells of "an old man whom infirmity and poverty have robbed of hope. What remains for him now is to await the last day of his life. All at once, however, he receives word of a great inheritance." The news causes an unexpected change in him: "immediately he forgets his anxieties and thinks of nothing else but the news. His spirit grows stronger as a result of this unexpected joy and his vigour returns." The *Pastor* concludes: "The same is true in your case, having seen all these good things, your heart has regained its youth."[79]

---

[73] Cf. 2 Cor 4:10.
[74] Cf. 1 Cor 15:1-53.
[75] Rm 12:12.
[76] SAINT BASIL THE GREAT, *Homily on Thanksgiving*, 3.
[77] Rm 15:13.
[78] Rm 5:5.
[79] PASTOR OF HERMES, *Vision* III, 20-21.

Continuing on the same subject, Pascal offers the following: "We do not require great education of the mind to understand that in this world there is no real and lasting satisfaction; that our pleasures are only vanity; that our evils are infinite; and, lastly, that death, which threatens us at every moment, must infallibly place us, within a few years, under the dreadful necessity of being for ever either annihilated or unhappy. There is nothing more real than this, nothing more terrible. As heroic as we might like to be, that is the end which awaits the world. Let us reflect on this and then ask ourselves whether it is not beyond doubt that there is no good in this life except having the hope of another life; that we are happy only in proportion to our drawing near it; and that, as there are no more woes for those who have complete assurance of eternity, so there is no happiness for those who have no insight into it."[80]

Surely, happiness is significantly threatened by the precarious nature of human existence: life has "the nature of a fleeting moment."[81] The certainty of the resurrection is the only foundation for Christian joy.

Hope gives joy its definitive character, since the believer is made to consider the glorious world destined for the future. Christian joy always bears the mark of Easter, because it awaits in "blessed hope" the fulfilment of the promise made by the Risen Christ.[82]

---

[80]   BLAISE PASCAL, *Pensées*, 194.
[81]   S. NATOLI, *La felicità. Saggio di teoria degli affetti* ("Happiness. Articles on the Affective Nature of Man"), Feltrinelli, Milano 1994, p. 13.
[82]   Cf. Titus 2:13.

MARIANI CESARE (1826-1901)

The stoning of Paul in Lystra (Acts 14: 19-20)

3. "Rejoice in your hope, be patient in tribulation" [83]

For Paul, the major obstacle to joy is the internal state of humankind after original sin: "For I know that nothing good dwells within me , that is, in my flesh. I can will what is right, but I cannot do it. For I do not do the good I want, but the evil I do not want is what I do. Now if I do what I do not want, it is no longer I that do it, but sin which dwells within me. So I find it to be a law that when I want to do right, evil lies close at hand. For I delight in the law of God, in my inmost self, but I see in my members another law at war with the law of my mind and making me captive to the law of sin, which dwells in my members." [84]

In the Letter to the Romans, the Apostle writes: "where sin increased, grace abounded all the more." [85] The Lord personally assured him: "My grace is sufficient for you." [86] The grace of God liberates him from this struggle, giving him the strength to choose good. [87]

For Jews and unbelievers alike, true blessedness consists in receiving the forgiveness of sins. [88] The one who acts with a right conscience, faithful to his convictions, is "blessed" (*makários*). [89]

The supreme principle for every action is charity. Paul strongly urges his hearers: "Rejoice in your hope, be patient in tribulation." [90] He reveals his

---

[83] Rm 12:12.

[84] Rm 7:18-23.

[85] Rm 5:20.

[86] 2 Cor 12:9.

[87] Cf. 1 Tm 1:13-14; 2 Tm 2:1.

[88] Cf. Rm 4:6-9. In this text, citing Psalm 31:1-2, the terms *makários* and *makarismós* appear twice.

[89] Cf. Rm 14:22.

[90] Rm 12:12

thinking on the subject; he is convinced that nothing can separate him from the joyous possession of the love of Christ, not tribulation, nor distress, nor persecution, nor hunger, nor nakedness, nor peril, nor the sword.[91]

Life's fair share of trials and sufferings is no reason to lose heart; forbearance will maintain peace within the soul and with others. What matters is to exercise a spirit of fellowship: "Rejoice with those who rejoice, weep with those who weep. Live in harmony with one another."[92]

Participating in the joy of others, increases it; sharing another's sorrow, diminishes it, even though the author of Proverbs states that such sharing is difficult, because the deepest sentiments of the heart are often beyond words: "The heart knows its own bitterness, and no stranger can share its joy."[93]

With particular eloquence, St. John Chrysostom comments in this matter: "to do this ('to weep with those who weep') nature itself reminds us: no one is so hard-hearted as not to weep over a person who is in misfortune. But the other ('to rejoice with those who rejoice') requires a very noble soul, not simply to resist the temptation to envy another's good fortune, but also to share another's pleasure. This is why Paul placed it first, for nothing so binds one to another as sharing both joy and sorrow. Therefore, do not let the absence of suffering in your own life keep you from sharing another's sorrow. For when your neighbour is ill-treated, you ought to make his problems your own. Share then in his tears, so that you might lighten his sagging spirit. Share in his joy, that joy might be more deeply rooted and love more firmly established. In so doing, you are the

---

[91]   Cf. Rm 8:35.
[92]   Rm 12:15-16.
[93]   Proverbs 14:10.

one who benefits the more; by your weeping you become merciful, and by sharing his pleasure, you purify yourself of envy and malice."[94]

Paul also refers to the manner in which the Christian ought to do good: "He who does acts of mercy, with cheerfulness (*hilaróteti*)."[95]

He insists on the interrelation of faith, peace, hope and joy. No joy can exist apart from communion with God, an optimistic outlook towards the future and good relations with others. With this spiritual attitude, the Christian experiences happiness. Such an understanding underlies the solemn wish which Paul addresses to the believers in Rome: "May the God of hope fill you with all joy and peace in believing, so that by the power of the Holy Spirit you may abound in hope."[96]

St. Augustine comments on the subject in the following manner: "Who rejoices in what is not seen? Is it not the Lord whom we see? This is the only object of promise. Now, instead, 'we walk by faith, while we are at home in the body we are away from the Lord.'[97] In faith and not by sight. You ask: 'When will we walk by sight?' When what John says is fulfilled: 'Beloved, we are God's children now; it does not yet appear what we shall be, but we know that when he appears we shall be like him, for we shall see him as he is.'[98] Great and perfect happiness will follow; there will be full joy, hope will no longer have need to sustain us, but the reality itself shall fill us. However, even now, before this reality comes about, before we reach that reality, let us rejoice in the Lord. No small joy comes from the hope which is focussed on this reality."[99]

---

[94] SAINT JOHN CHRYSOSTOM, *Homily on the Letter to the Romans*, 22, 1-2.

[95] Rm 12:8.

[96] Rm 15:13.

[97] 2 Cor 5:6-7.

[98] 1 Jn 3:2.

[99] SAINT AUGUSTINE, *Discourse XXI*, 1-4.

Though Paul had not yet seen the Romans, he intends to visit them "in joy." In the meantime, he extends the following wish: "The God of peace be with you all," as if to anticipate this sense of joy.[100]

A little earlier he stated: "We have peace with God through our Lord Jesus Christ."[101] In Christ God has shown his "love for us." Paul's reasoning in this regard is very clear: "if while we were enemies we were reconciled to God by the death of his Son, much more, now that we are reconciled, shall we be saved by his life. Not only so, but we also rejoice in God through our Lord Jesus Christ, through whom we have now received our reconciliation."[102]

Paul shares with the Romans a "great sorrow and increasing anguish in his heart,"[103] which threatens to eclipse his joy – the Jews' rejection of the Gospel. He has already "become all things to all men" so as to win over for the Gospel the greatest possible number of persons.[104] However, to do good to his "brothers, kinsmen by race" he would be willing to endure the most terrible of misfortunes: to be "anathema (accursed), cut off from Christ."[105] In an indirect and paradoxical manner, Paul states that his profound joy would be to renounce his personal joy, flowing from his intimate union with Christ, so that joy might come to those to whom he was sent.

In a post-script, after having sent a greeting to the Christians in Asia (Ephesus), the bearers of his letter to the Church in Rome, who are his coworkers, kinsmen and friends, Paul writes: "I rejoice over you," because "your obedience is known to all."[106]

---

[100] Rm 15:32.
[101] Rm 5:1.
[102] Rm 5:8,10-11.
[103] Rm 9:2.
[104] 1 Cor 9:22.
[105] Rm 9:3.
[106] Rm 16:19.

Paul's speech in the Aeropagus of Athens (*Acts* 17:22-34)

4. "The fruit of the spirit is joy" [107]

In the Letter to the Galatians, Paul recalls with emotion the great generosity extended to him during his illness: "if possible, you would have plucked out your eyes and given them to me;"[108] and his astonishment that they wish "to accept another Gospel,"[109] making him ironically say: "What has become of the satisfaction (*makarismós*) you felt?"[110]

He then relates that "the fruit of the Spirit is love, joy, peace, patience, kindness, goodness, faithfulness, gentleness, self-control."[111] Joy is the dominant note in the concert of virtues. So as not to create disharmony, one must also "crucify the flesh with its passions and desires" and "walk by the Spirit."[112]

The Apostle wrote to the Corinthians: "For the word of the cross is folly to those who are perishing, but to us who are being saved it is the power of God. ... we preach Christ crucified, a stumbling block to Jews and folly to Gentiles."[113] Convinced that joy flows from suffering, he now tells the Galatians: "But far be it from me to glory except in the cross of our Lord Jesus Christ, by which the world has been crucified to me, and I to the world."[114]

---

[107] Gal 5:22.
[108] Gal 4:15.
[109] Gal 1:6.
[110] Gal 4:15.
[111] Gal 5:22.
[112] Gal 5:24-25.
[113] 1 Cor 1:18,23.
[114] Gal 6:14.

St. Cyril of Jerusalem (ca. 315-387), re-echoing Paul's words, states that "the cross is the glory of all glories."[115]

---

[115] SAINT CYRIL OF JERUSALEM, *Baptismal Catechesis*, 13, 1.

Paul and Silas are flogged in Philippi (Acts 16: 16-24)

5.   "Rejoice always in the Lord" [116]

The Letter to the Philippians is rightly called the "letter of joy." Paul, after having wished "grace and peace to all the saints in Jesus Christ who are at Philippi," sends reassurance that he is "carrying them in his heart" and has "a deep affection" for them all. In this regard, he sends these special words: "I thank my God in all my remembrance of you, always in every prayer of mine for you all, making my prayer with joy, thankful for your partnership in the Gospel from the first day until now."[117] He is happy that the Gospel has spread and that believers are experiencing its benefits and persevering in the faith which they have embraced. He also voices contentment that his work was not in vain.

Some in the community have zealously dedicated themselves to evangelization in order to demonstrate to Paul that even in his absence the work of the Gospel continues. At one time he spoke of "false brothers,"[118] but now he is more understanding and limits himself to making the observation that what counts is reaching out to people, without judging intentions of who is more or less right: "Only that in every way, whether in pretence or in truth, Christ is proclaimed; and in that I rejoice." [119] The Apostle's joy finds its source in his faith and mission. It is of little importance if evangelization continues through others, because he

---

[116]   Phil 4:4.
[117]   Phil 1:1-5,7-8.
[118]   Cf. 2 Cor 11:26; Gal 2:4.
[119]   Phil 1:18.

is "in chains like a criminal." His interior peace cannot be disturbed, as he serenely states that "the Word of God is not fettered."[120]

Despite the fact that Paul was "fortunate" (*makários*) in having the possibility of defending himself against the accusations of the Jews before King Agrippa,[121] he is taken to Rome as a prisoner.[122] Though unable to do much from prison, he is convinced of surviving to continue "to be a help" to his faithful "for the progress and joy of their faith."[123] His linking of joy and faith shows the connection between the two. Faith fills the spirit with comfort, tranquillity, peace, the strength of endurance and courage. Both believing and suffering are paradoxically a "grace" of God.[124] For some, suffering can be the reason for distancing themselves from God. However, for those who know how to accept it, suffering can strengthen their faith.

Paul desires that the joy he experiences, because of the faithful of Philippi, might increase: "So if there is any encouragement in Christ, any incentive of love, any participation in the Spirit, any affection and sympathy, complete my joy by being of the same mind, having the same love, being in full accord and of one mind."[125] Bernanos rightly observes: "To know how to reap joy in the joy of others is the secret of happiness."[126]

At the very moment that Paul is far away and in prison, he can rejoice in knowing that the

---

[120] 2 Tim 2:9.
[121] Cf. Acts 26:2.
[122] Cf. Acts 27:1.
[123] Phil 1:25.
[124] Cf. Phil 1:29.
[125] Phil 2:1-2.
[126] GEORGE BERNANOS, *La joie* ("Joy"), 583.

community is persevering in fraternal charity. His insistence on unity, however, leads one to believe that the community was threatened by divisions.[127] He therefore mentions that charity cannot be exercised without humility, as Jesus taught in his own life: "And being found in human form, he humbled himself and became obedient unto death, even death on a cross."[128] This sad lament indicates how much he takes its message to heart, not so much for the comfort he could derive from it as much as for the testimony of love which believers ought to render, if they wish to be seen as followers of Christ.[129]

Paul declares that he is ready joyously to accept even martyrdom and to be offered as an oblation for the sake "of the glorious Gospel of the blessed God with which I have been entrusted;"[130] "Even if I am to be poured as a libation upon the sacrificial offering of your faith, I am glad and rejoice with you all. Likewise you also should be glad and rejoice with me."[131]

St. Polycarp addressed these words to the Philippians: "I rejoice greatly with you in our Lord Jesus Christ that you have followed the pattern of true love, and have helped on their way, as opportunity was given you, those who were bound in chains, which become the saints, and are the diadems of those who have been truly chosen by God and our Lord. I rejoice also that your firmly rooted faith, which was famous in past years, still flourishes and bears fruit unto our Lord Jesus Christ."[132]

---

[127] Cf. Phil 1:15-17, 27; 2:14; 4:2.
[128] Phil 2:8.
[129] Cf. Jn 13:35.
[130] 1 Tim 1:11.
[131] Phil 2:17-18.
[132] SAINT POLYCARP, *Letter to the Philippians*, 1, 1.

The Apostle reveals his deep-seated desire to achieve union with Christ, who lives in him,[133] and the joy this brings: "But whatever gain I had, I counted as loss for the sake of Christ. Indeed I count everything as loss because of the surpassing worth of knowing Christ Jesus my Lord. For his sake I have suffered the loss of all things, and count them as refuse, in order that I may gain Christ."[134] The obvious consequence of his action is: "For me to live is Christ, and to die is gain," because he burns with a "desire to depart and be with Christ."[135]

The community at Philippi stands in need of a visit from Paul, but he is physically impeded. Not even Timothy, a long acquaintance, is able to make the trip. Instead, the Apostle, "with all care," sends Epaphroditus for the following purpose: "that you may rejoice at seeing him again, and that I may be less anxious." Since the faithful are an isolated part of a large population, the visit of a special envoy brings them in touch with the Church throughout the world, thus reassuring them and lifting their spirits. What matters is the message, not the bearer as such. Paul therefore asks them to "receive him in the Lord with all joy."[136] Joy shows that they are of one mind with the Apostle who, in the last analysis, is of the same mind as Christ, the "blessed and only Sovereign."[137]

Joy is present in the heart of this prisoner of Christ more than any other concern: "Finally, my brethren, rejoice in the Lord."[138] He likewise states

---

[133] Cf. Gal 2:20.
[134] Phil 3:7-8.
[135] Phil 1:21, 23.
[136] Phil 2:28-29.
[137] 1 Tim 6:15.
[138] Phil 3:1.

in a more affectionate manner: "My brethren, who I love and long for, my joy and crown, stand firm, thus in the Lord, my beloved."[139]

Distance and prison bars bring out many emotions in Paul, making him repeat himself in many words; but their ultimate meaning is always the same – a lively satisfaction at how the young community which he founded remains faithful to the Gospel message.

As in the case of the Thessalonians, the Philippians are even now for Paul – almost in anticipation of what is to be fulfilled in the last days – "the crown of righteousness" which the Lord will give him, after he has "fought the good fight and finished the race."[140] In this regard, Beaupère rightly observes: "The term 'crown' does not indicate that joy is purely psychological. The joy of the Apostle is not principally his personal state of mind, but the realization that God gives a vocation its fullness and definitive joyousness."[141]

His appeal then becomes more urgent: "Rejoice in the Lord always; again I will say, Rejoice."[142] All anxieties and daily difficulties need to be gathered and entrusted to the Lord who is near.[143]

St. John Chrysostom responds to the question which Paul's plea might cause: "To rejoice for a time is no hard matter, but to rejoice con-

---

[139] Phil 4:1.
[140] 2 Tim 4:7-8.
[141] N. BEAUPÈRE, *San Paolo e la gioia, op. cit.* ("St. Paul and Joy"), p. 58.
[142] Phil 4:4. This verse served as the inspiration for the title of the Paul VI's Apostolic Exhortation on joy: *Gaudete in Domino* (9 May 1975).
[143] Cf. Phil 4:5-6.

tinually, this seems to me to be impossible. For many are the causes of sadness, which surround us on all sides. A man has lost either a son, or a wife, or a beloved friend, more necessary to him than all kindred; or he has to sustain the loss of wealth; or he has fallen into sickness; or he has to bear some other change of fortune; or to grieve for contemptuous treatment which he did not deserve; or famine, or pestilence, or some intolerable exaction, or circumstances in his family trouble him; – nay, there is no saying how many circumstances of a public or private nature are accustomed to bring us grief. How then, he may say, is it possible to "rejoice always?"

The secret is contained in the Apostle's own words. Indeed, "He does not simply say, 'Rejoice always;' but he adds the cause of sustaining this good pleasure, saying, 'Rejoice in the Lord always.' He who rejoices 'in the Lord,' cannot be deprived of this pleasure by anything that may happen. For all other things in which we rejoice are passing and changeable, and subject to variation."[144]

To bring Paul to "rejoice greatly in the Lord,"[145] it is enough for him to know that the Philippians again manifest the sentiments which they have always had in his regard.

---

[144] SAINT JOHN CHRYSOSTOM, *Homilies Concerning the Statues*, XVIII, 3, 6.
[145] Phil 4:10.

GRANDI FRANCESCO (1831-1891)

Paul is expelled from the Temple (*Acts* 21: 26-40)

6.   "I have derived much joy and comfort from your love" [146]

The appeal for joy is also a dominating factor in the Letter to Philemon. Paul, now "an old man and a prisoner for Jesus Christ," [147] writing with his own hand, [148] asks Philemon, his "beloved fellow worker" and "brother" [149] to give him the "pleasure" (*onáimen*) of fraternally receiving into his house as if it were himself, [150] the runaway slave Onesimus, "whose father he became in his imprisonment." [151]

Paul, hearing others speak of the charity which Philemon has "toward the Lord Jesus and all the saints," [152] states that he needs to be the recipient of the same benevolence which has brought him such renown: "For I derived much joy and comfort from your love, my brother, because the hearts of the saints have been refreshed through you." [153] Joy comes, above all, from good works which lighten another's burden.

---

[146]   Philemon 7.
[147]   Philemon 9; cf. 1.
[148]   Cf. Philemon 19.
[149]   Philemon 1.
[150]   Philemon 17.
[151]   Philemon 10.
[152]   Philemon 5.
[153]   Philemon 7.

Paul before Felix in Caesarea (*Acts*, 23: 34-24, 27)

7. "I rejoice in my sufferings for your sake" [154]

The author of the Letter to the Colossians urges the Church community to give thanks "with joy to the Father, who has qualified us to share in the inheritance of the saints in light. He has delivered us from the dominion of darkness and transferred us to the kingdom of his beloved Son, in whom we have redemption, the forgiveness of sins." [155]

A reflection follows on the apparently opposing elements in the apostle's mission: "Now I rejoice in my sufferings for your sake, and in my flesh I complete what is lacking in Christ's afflictions for the sake of his body, that is, the church." [156] At a later date he will confide in Timothy: "I endure everything for the sake of the elect, that they also may obtain the salvation which in Christ Jesus goes with eternal glory." [157]

Two concepts – joy and suffering – which normally appear irreconcilable are for Paul a synthesis of the Christian's life and activity. "Sufferings" are the troubles and concerns which the missionary must to face in proclaiming the Gospel. Their association with the passion of Christ and the benefit which can come to the brethren explains how joy can be had amidst suffering.

This is very clearly revealed in the life of St. Ignatius of Antioch, who was condemned to death under the Emperor Trajan (98-178 A.D.). On this occasion he reminds the faithful of Philadelphia that the passion of Christ fills the Church with joy. [158] He writes to the Church in Smyrna that "we are the fruit of his divinely blessed passion" and that the meaning of the passion is

---

[154] Col 1:24.
[155] Col 1:12-14.
[156] Col 1:24.
[157] 2 Tim 2:10.
[158] Cf. SAINT IGNATIUS OF ANTIOCH, *Letter to the Philadelphians*, Introduction.

understood by its effects: peace, joy and election.[159] For Polycarp, who was martyred about 156 A.D., joy is the gift of being gratuitously saved through Christ.[160]

When faced with death, as in the case of Polycarp and the many other martyrs, joy makes the Christian's face shine. This is perhaps the very reason why a Christian's death is a witness which always elicits a reaction and is capable of either attracting or scandalizing.[161] In this regard, it suffices to recall the witness of the martyrs of Lyons. St. Irenaeus, who as a youth knew St. Polycarp, gives the following account: "...comforted by the joy of martyrdom, the hope and promise of blessedness and the love of Christ and the Spirit of the Father, ... they happily went forth, uplifted in spirit and covered with glory and grace; their chains appeared like adornments and signs of distinction, like rings of gold on the hands of a spouse."[162]

Paul writes to the Colossians while confined to prison,[163] yet he is not downcast in spirit, because "though I am absent in body, yet I am with you in spirit, rejoicing to see your good order and the firmness of your faith in Christ."[164]

In seeking joy, Christians ought primarily to bear in mind the demands of the "new life" given them by Christ: "If then you have been raised with Christ, seek the things that are above, where Christ is seated at the right hand of God. Set your minds on things that are above, not on things that are on earth."[165] Jesus explicitly said: "Seek first his kingdom and his righteousness, and all these things (material benefits) shall be yours as well."[166]

---

[159] SAINT IGNATIUS OF ANTIOCH, *Letter to the Smyrnaeans*, 1.

[160] Cf. SAINT POLYCARP, *Letter to the Philippians*, 1.

[161] Cf. *Martyrdom of Polycarp*, 12.

[162] *Martyrdom of St. Plotinus and the Martyrs of Lyons, X.*

[163] Cf. Col 4:10.

[164] Col 2:5.

[165] Col 3:1-2.

[166] Matt 6:33.

BARTOLINI DOMENICO

Paul's shipwreck in Cauda (*Acts* 27: 1-44)

8. "For the moment all seems painful rather than pleasant" [167]

When the Christian's sufferings are borne for others they can be accepted with joy. The author of the Letter to the Hebrews has the same message: "But recall the former days when, after you were enlightened, you endured a hard struggle with sufferings, sometimes being publicly exposed to abuse and affliction, and sometimes being partners with those so treated. For you had compassion on the prisoners, and you joyfully accepted the plundering of your property, since you knew that you yourselves had a better possession and an abiding one." [168]

Former Jewish priests were probably among the intended recipients of this letter, since they were known to react angrily to injustices, consigning their adversaries to God's wrath. The gentle, submissive attitude which they now displayed is authentic proof of their conversion.

The Christian adds a new dimension to life from which his present and future are put into perspective. The capacity joyously to accept the loss of goods comes from the conviction that such a loss is the price of salvation, the supreme good. But the ultimate reason for the believer's actions is always Jesus Christ, the model necessarily to be followed in living the faith: "He, for the joy that was set before him

---

[167] Heb 12:11.
[168] Heb 10:32-34

endured the cross, despising the shame, and is seated at the right hand of the throne of God."[169] Jesus renounced the easy joy of success proposed by the tempter.[170] "He was rich but became poor."[171] "He died for us."[172]

Following the example of Christ, sorrow and joy are inseparable bywords in the Christian's life. Surely, suffering is opposed to human nature. However, given a meaning, it can be transformed into joy.

The pedagogic value of correction can further clarify this thought: "For the moment all discipline seems painful rather than pleasant; later it yields the peaceful fruit of righteousness to those who have been trained by it"[173] Suffering, if accepted as part of the providential plan of God, allows the Christian to grow, makes his choice more solid and satisfying and becomes the source of serenity and peace.

The author of the Letter to the Hebrews is evidently a pastor of souls, when he calls for perfect understanding between the leaders and faithful of the community. One must know how to lead, the others how to follow. The bond uniting the dual actions of overseeing and putting into action comes from a humility and joy, which precludes displeasing reactions from one or the other: "Obey your leaders and submit to them; for they are keeping watch over your souls, as men who will have to give account. Let them do this joyfully, and not

---

[169] Heb 12:2.
[170] Cf. Matt 4:1-11.
[171] 2 Cor 8:9.
[172] 1 Titus 5:10.
[173] Heb 12:11.

sadly, for that would be of no advantage to you."[174]

Where Paul's language and theological framework is open to discussion, his message on joy is not: Only the God-man, Jesus Christ, offers the path to truth, well-being, peace and joy: "For all the promises of God find their yes in him. That is why we utter the Amen through him, to the glory of God."[175]

---

[174] Heb 13:17
[175] 2 Cor 1:20.

Index